MACMILLAN/McGRAW-HILL

# Language Arts

AUTHORS

Jan E. Hasbrouck

Donna Lubcker

Sharon O'Neal

William H. Teale

Josefina V. Tinajero

Karen D. Wood

# Table of Contents

UNIT

## 1 Open Your Eyes!

Concepts of Print/ Readiness

UNIT

## 2 Hand in Hand

Nouns

## Every Unit Includes:

- Oral Language
- Shared Reading
- Grammar
- Comprehension
- Study Skills
- Writing

## UNIT 3 Tell Me About It

Verbs

## UNIT 4 What's New?

Sentences

# UNIT 5 Put On Your Thinking Cap

Describing Words

# UNIT 6 Pick a Plan

Pronouns

# Open Your Eyes!

UNIT 1

Name ____________________

**UNIT 1 OPENER** • Draw a picture of a pet you would like to have.

Name

 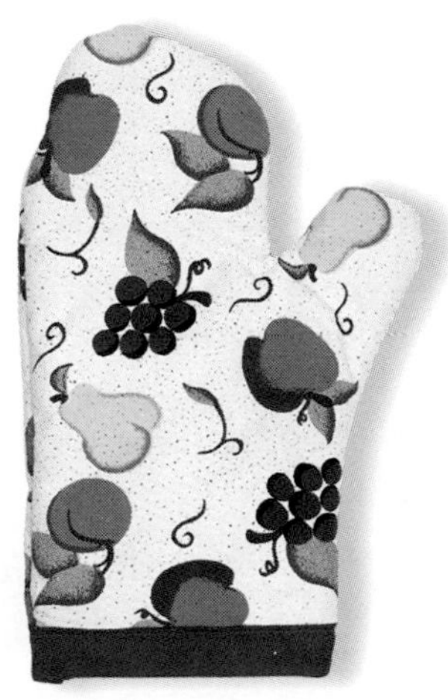 

**SAME AND DIFFERENT** • Draw a circle around the two pictures in each row that are the same. • Draw a line under the picture that is different.

**EXTEND** Draw three cookies. Make two the same and one different.

**AT HOME** Think of two things that are the same and draw a picture of them.

Name

SAME AND DIFFERENT • Look at the pictures in each box. • Draw a line to connect the two pictures that are the same.

EXTEND Study the pictures of the frog and toad. Tell how they are the same, as well as different.

AT HOME Draw pictures of three teddy bears. Make two bears the same, and one different.

Name______________________________ READ TOGETHER

rake rake shovel rake

bagel muffin bagel bagel

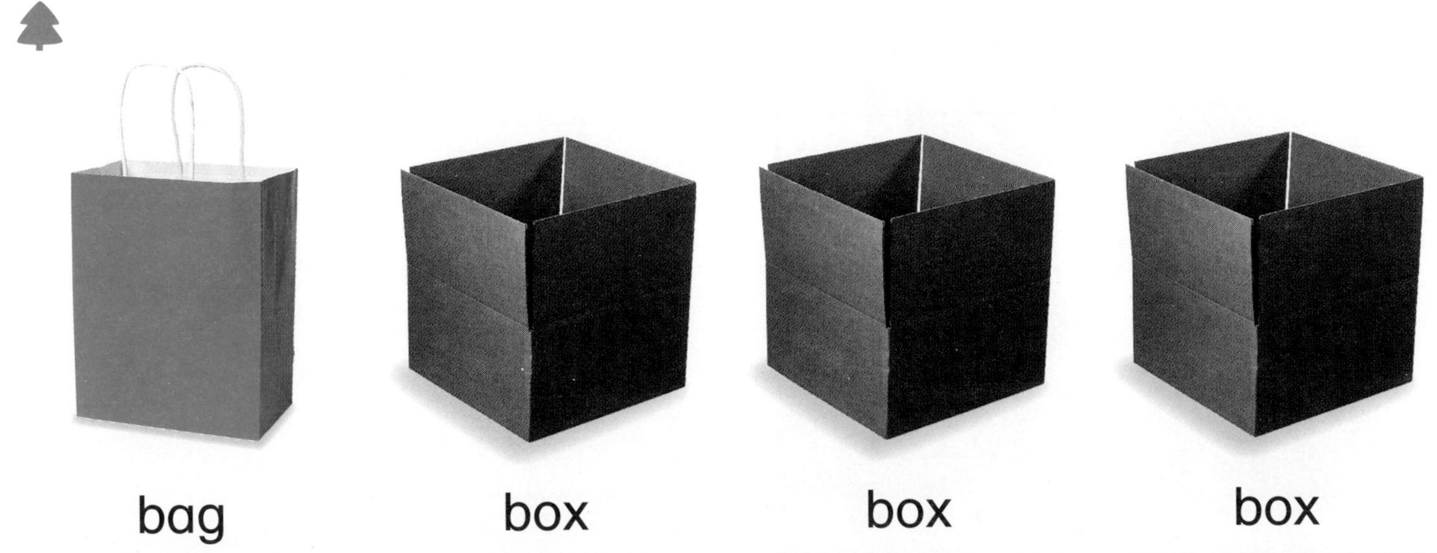

bag box box box

**SAME AND DIFFERENT** Look at the pictures in each row. • Then draw a circle around the picture that is different.

**EXTEND** Draw pictures of two things in the classroom that are alike. Label your pictures.

**AT HOME** Find two things that are alike. Draw pictures of the things you find.

Name

**MAKING LISTS** • The pictures on the left show three "delicious wishes" from the poem. • Tell what each picture shows. • Then, in the boxes on the right, make your own picture list of three wishes.

**EXTEND** Take turns telling about your list of wishes.

**AT HOME** Make a wish for each person in your family. Draw a picture to show what you wished.

Name____________________

Aa Nn Dd

Ss Mm Ii

Tt Cc Oo

Ff Rr Pp

**CAPITAL AND LOWERCASE LETTERS** • Name each pair of letters. Draw a circle around the capital letters. Draw a circle around the lowercase letters.

**EXTEND** Underline the letters in your name that are also on this page.

**AT HOME** Point out and name the letters you know on a page in a book or magazine.

Name

A

p

G

d

P

a

D

g

McGraw-Hill School Division

**CAPITAL AND LOWERCASE LETTERS** • Look at each picture and the letter next to it. • Draw a line to match each capital letter with its lowercase letter.

**EXTEND** Draw a fox and a baby fox and label them with Ff.

**AT HOME** Cut out from magazines two capital and lowercase letters that match.

Name________________________________ READ TOGETHER

S s

C c

M m

R r

**CAPITAL AND LOWERCASE LETTERS** • Look at each sign and the letters below it. • Find the capital and lowercase form of the same letter in the sign. • Draw a circle around the letters.

**EXTEND** Look in a book for words with these letters: M and i; P and r; S and o. Write the words.

**AT HOME** Find these letters at home: Ff, Aa, Cc, Tt. Look on boxes and labels in the kitchen.

Name ___________________________________________

USE ILLUSTRATIONS • Draw a red circle around the main character in the story. • Draw a blue circle around the animal who helped the main character. • Then change the picture of the littlest reindeer to show how it looked at the end of the story.

EXTEND Make a picture list of your favorite animals. Label your pictures.

AT HOME Use the picture on this page to help you tell someone the story of the littlest reindeer.

Name

Kk Gg Uu

Ee Bb Ll

Hh Ww Yy

Jj Zz Qq

**CAPITAL AND LOWERCASE LETTERS** • Name the letters. Draw a circle around each lowercase letter. Draw a circle around each capital letter.

**EXTEND** Underline and count the lowercase letters in your name.

**AT HOME** Take turns picking out lowercase and uppercase letters in the newspaper.

Name___________________________________ READ TOGETHER

Seals

Turtles

Baboons

Eagles

Rhinoceroses

Porcupines

**CAPITAL AND LOWERCASE LETTERS** • Look at the word below each picture as your teacher reads the word. • Draw a circle around the first letter in the word. • Then find and circle the matching lowercase letter in the word.

**EXTEND** Find matching capital and lowercase letters in magazines. Cut them out.

**AT HOME** Look for B and b on labels and boxes. Cut and paste them on paper.

Name_______________________________________________

y  u

E K O

T E B

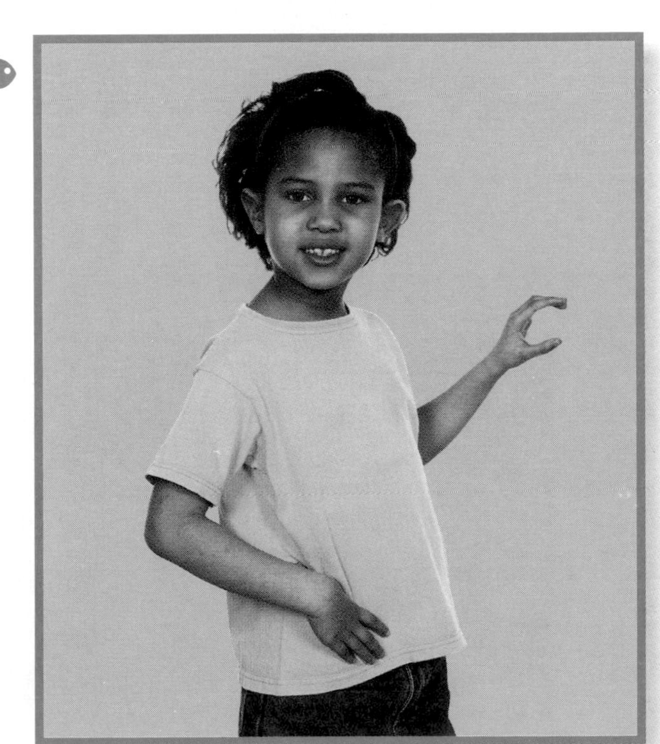

h g c

**CAPITAL AND LOWERCASE LETTERS** • Look at each picture. • What letter is the child forming? • Draw a circle around the correct letter below the picture.

**EXTEND** With a partner, think of ways to form these letters with your fingers or bodies: E, L, b, U, k, g.

**AT HOME** Find these capital and lowercase letters in a newspaper: W, w, H, h, B, b, E, e.

Name________________________________ READ TOGETHER

duck

pony

rabbit

**USE ILLUSTRATIONS** • Draw a circle around which pet in each row you think the person in the poem might like better. • Draw a line under the pet you would rather have.

**EXTEND** Think of reasons why both real and stuffed animals make good pets.

**AT HOME** Make a picture list of toy animals you have.

Name

**LEFT TO RIGHT** • Tell where each child in the picture is going. • Trace each child's path from left to right.

**EXTEND** Draw pictures of your right hand and left hand. Label the pictures.

**AT HOME** Trace which hand you use to eat and to write. Tell which hand it is.

Name ____________________

**LEFT TO RIGHT** Draw a line from the left glove to the right glove. Draw a line from the left mitten to the right mitten. Draw a line from the left shoe to the right shoe.

**EXTEND** With a partner, make a list of all things that come in left-and-right pairs, like hands and feet.

**AT HOME** Have someone help you trace your hands. Write **L** on the left hand and **R** on the right.

Name________________________ READ TOGETHER

fire truck

firehouse

train

train station

mail truck

post office

**LEFT TO RIGHT** • Draw a line to show where each vehicle is going. • Go from left to right.

**EXTEND** Imagine yourself in one of the vehicles on this page. Draw a picture to show where you would go.

**AT HOME** Draw a picture of something else that is going from left to right. Tell where it is going.

Name________________________________________ READ TOGETHER

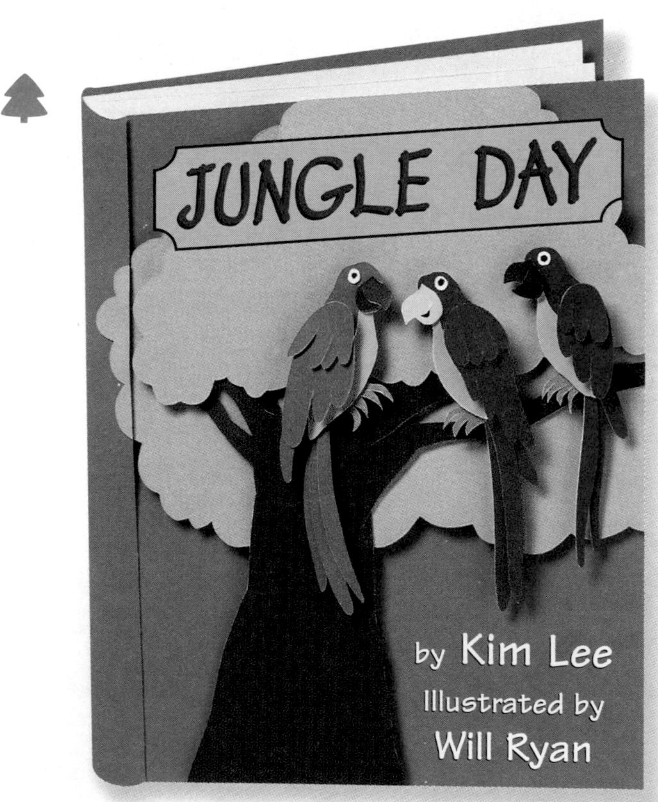


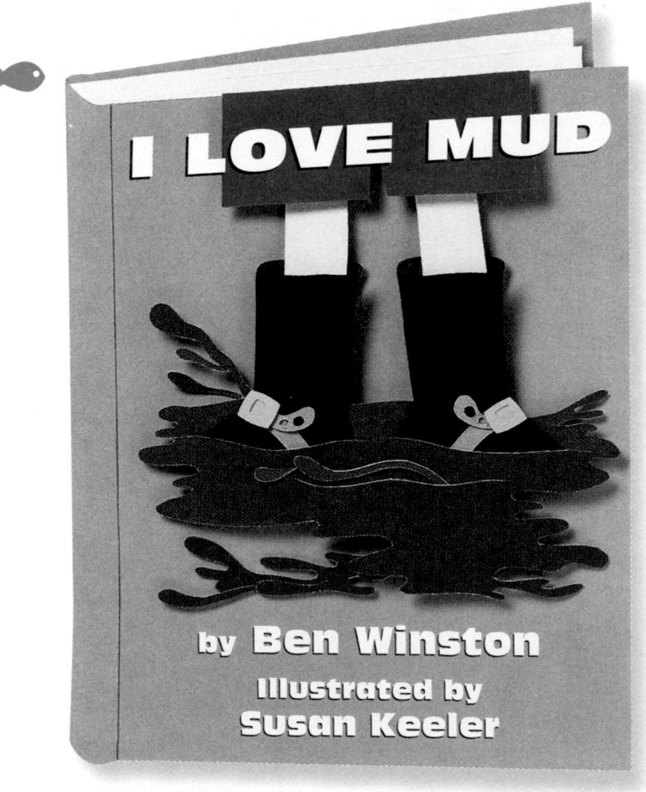

**PARTS OF A BOOK** • Draw a line under the words that tell the title of each book. • Draw a circle around the names of the authors and illustrators.

**EXTEND** Draw a picture that you think you might find inside one of the books on this page.

**AT HOME** Make your own book cover. Draw a picture that shows what your book is about.

Name ____________________

**CATEGORIES** • Tell where the girl will put her coat, boots, book, and teddy bear. • Draw a circle around each place you name.

**EXTEND** Draw a picture of a toy. Tell where it belongs in the photograph.

**AT HOME** Tell where you put your pajamas and your toothbrush at home.

Name

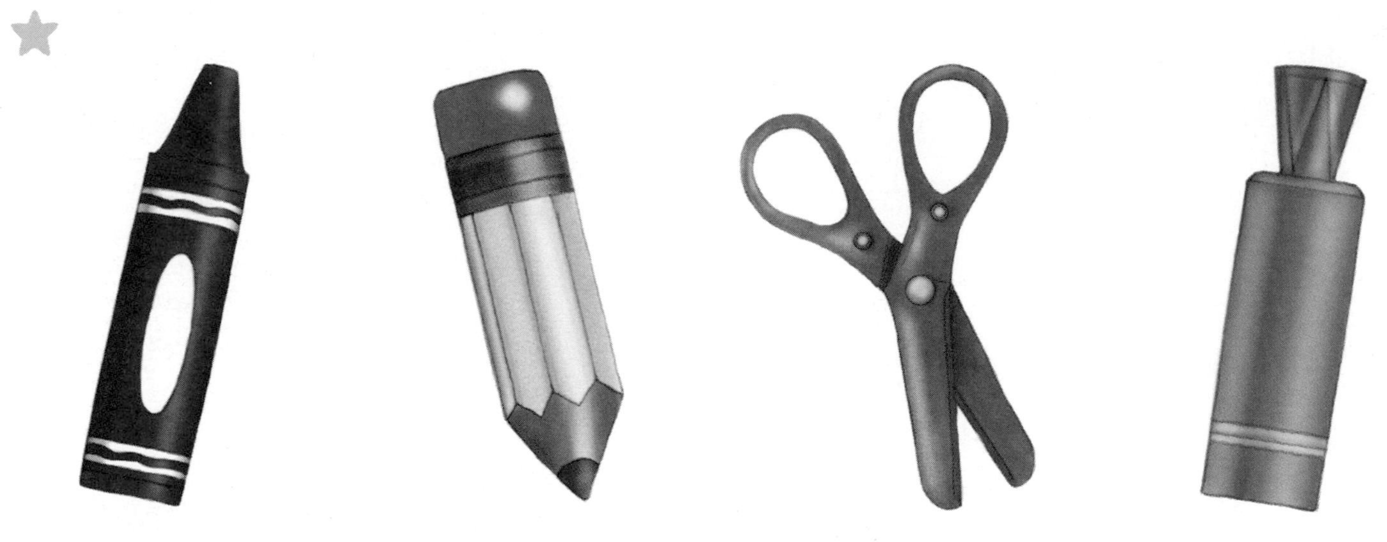

McGraw-Hill School Division

**CATEGORIES** Look at the pictures in each row. • Draw a circle around the picture that does not belong. Look at the shapes of the objects. • Draw a circle around the shape that does not belong.

**EXTEND** Think of at least two more things that fit in each of the categories.

**AT HOME** Find three things in your home that are hard. Draw pictures to show what you found.

Name ____________________ READ TOGETHER

car

train

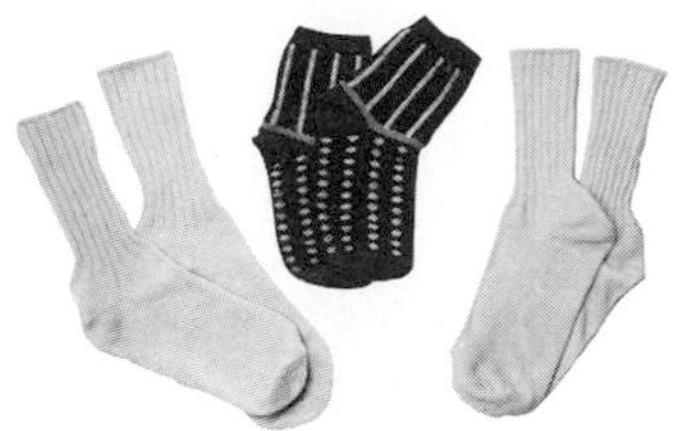

socks

van

teddy bear

ball

monkey

snake

coat

hat

kite

boots

**CATEGORIES** • Draw a circle around the picture that doesn't belong.

**EXTEND** Think about how the things in each row are the same. Draw another thing that fits the category.

**AT HOME** Find three things in your house that go together. Draw a picture of them.

Name ____________________ READ TOGETHER

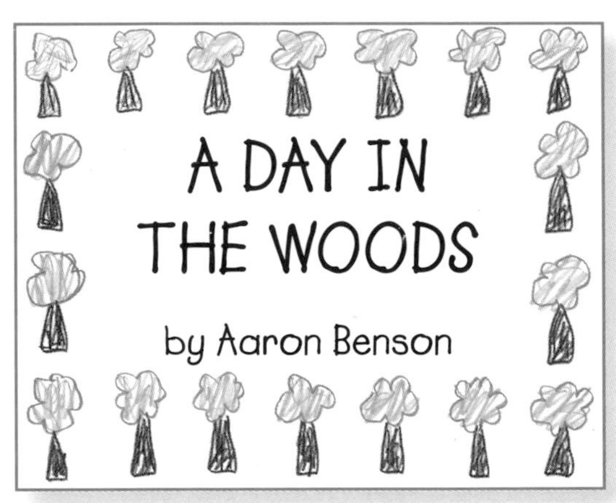

**PARTS OF A BOOK** • Look at the book covers on the left. • Draw a line from each cover to the title page that matches it.

**EXTEND** Make a cover for a book you would like to write.

**AT HOME** Make up your own story about a favorite animal. Make a cover for your story.

Name______________________________

**UNIT 1 WRAP-UP: Review Concepts of Print/ Readiness** • Draw a circle around the two things in each row that are the same.

Name________________________________

**UNIT 1 WRAP-UP: Draw Pictures** • Draw three animals you could see outside.

# Hand in Hand

UNIT 2

Name

**UNIT 2 OPENER** • Draw a picture of yourself at a picnic. • Show something you might do to help.

Name________________________________________

Mrs. Ryan
Andrew
Olivia
Marco
Anthony

**SPECIAL NOUNS THAT NAME PEOPLE**
• Draw a circle around the names of five people in the pictures. • Say the name that would be on your name tag if you were in the picture.

**EXTEND** Draw a picture of yourself and a friend. Label your picture with your names.

**AT HOME** Draw a picture of someone. Say the name of the person you have drawn.

Name

**SPECIAL NOUNS THAT NAME PEOPLE**
• Think about the poem "Lunch in a Line." • Draw a circle around the name tag of each person who helped make lunch. • Say the name of each person you circled.

**EXTEND** With a partner, try to remember the names of all the children who helped make lunch.

**AT HOME** Tell a story about people working together. Use the names of people you know.

Name ______________________________

**SPECIAL NOUNS THAT NAME PEOPLE** • Point out the people in each picture. • Draw circles around their name tags.

**EXTEND** Draw a picture of yourself. Label the picture with your name.

**AT HOME** Draw a picture of someone in your family. Say the noun that names the person you have drawn.

Name ______________________________

**SEQUENCE** • Draw a red circle around the picture that shows what happened first. • Draw a blue circle around the picture that shows what happened next. • Draw a green circle around the picture that shows what happened last.

**EXTEND** Draw pictures of three things your class does each day. Put them in order: first, next, last.

**AT HOME** Draw pictures that show what you do first in the morning and last at night.

Name ____________________

**SPECIAL NOUNS THAT NAME PEOPLE**

- Draw a circle around the person in each picture.
- Say the noun that names each person you circled.

**EXTEND** Draw someone who helps you in school. Label the person with the appropriate noun.

**AT HOME** Think of another noun that names a person. Draw a picture of the person.

Name

**NOUNS THAT NAME PEOPLE** • Draw a line from Old Mother Hubbard to each person she went to see. • Say the noun that tells what the person is or does.

**EXTEND** Memorize one or more verses of "Old Mother Hubbard." Act them out with friends.

**AT HOME** Use words to name people in your family, such as *sister*, *aunt*, *grandfather*.

Name

READ TOGETHER

baker truck letter carrier

firefighter astronaut lamp

cow dancer doctor

**NOUNS THAT NAME PEOPLE** • Draw a circle around the two people in each row. • Say the noun that tells who each person is.

**EXTEND** Draw a picture of a person doing a job in your town. Write the noun that names the person.

**AT HOME** Draw a picture of a job you might like someday. Say the word that tells what you are.

Name

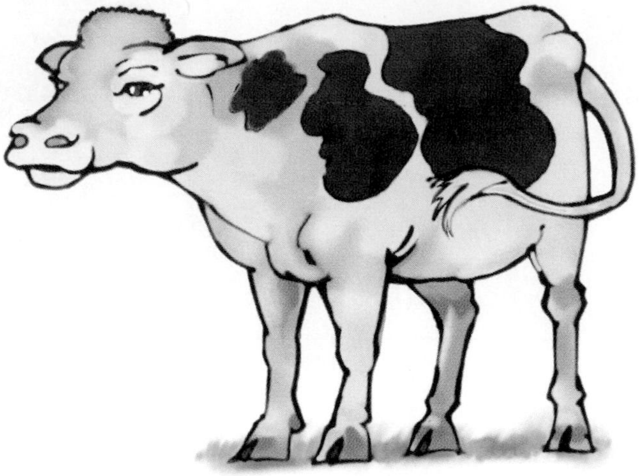

**SEQUENCE** • Draw a red line to the character the mouse went to first. • Draw a blue line to the character the mouse went to second. • Draw a green line to the character the mouse went to third. • Draw a yellow line to the character the mouse went to fourth.

**EXTEND** With some of your classmates, act out the story of "The Cat and the Mouse."

**AT HOME** Use the pictures on this page to retell the story of "The Cat and the Mouse."

Name

**NOUNS THAT NAME ANIMALS AND THINGS**

- Draw a circle around the animals in the pictures.
- Then name one thing you might find in each picture.

**EXTEND** Draw a picture of an animal. Label your picture with the noun that names your animal.

**AT HOME** Draw a picture of an animal. Tell a story using the noun that names your animal.

Name

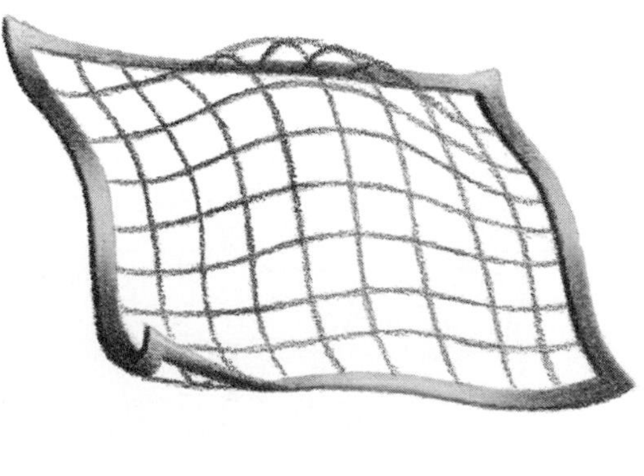



**NOUNS THAT NAME ANIMALS AND THINGS**
• Draw a circle around each animal or thing from the story. • Say the noun that names each one.

**EXTEND** Draw a picture with animals. Write the noun for each animal below its picture.

**AT HOME** Draw a picture for the story and label it with nouns for the animals.

Name________________________ READ TOGETHER

giraffe

girl

bookbag

man

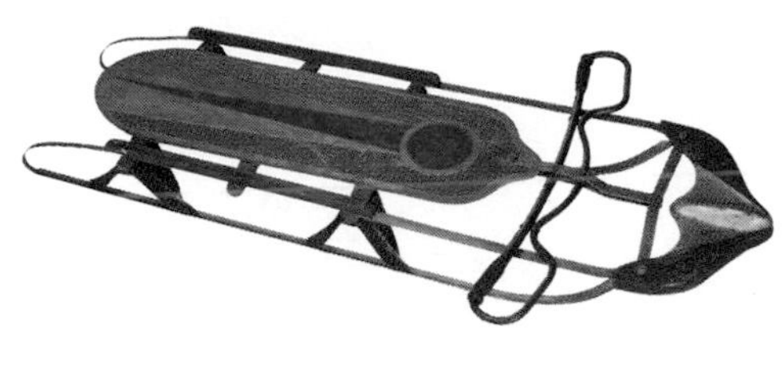
sled

seal

pig

chair

boy

**NOUNS THAT NAME ANIMALS AND THINGS**
• Draw a circle around each animal. • Draw a line under each thing. • Say the noun that names the animal or thing.

**EXTEND** Draw a picture of an animal and write the noun that tells what it is.

**AT HOME** Draw a picture of one animal and one thing. Tell the nouns that name them.

Name________________________________ READ TOGETHER

coyote

buffalo

eagle



**SIGNS/LABELS** • Find the picture of the buffalo. • Draw a red circle around its label. • Find the picture of the eagle. • Draw a blue circle around its label. • Find the picture of the coyote. • Draw a green circle around its label.

**EXTEND** Draw a picture of an animal from the story. Write a label below it.

**AT HOME** In your kitchen, find labels that name foods.

Name

**NOUNS THAT NAME PLACES** ● Draw red circles around the flower shop and the park. • Draw green circles around the restaurant and the market. ★ Draw red circles around the post office and the library. • Draw green circles around the playground and the firehouse.

**EXTEND** Draw your favorite place and write the noun that tells what it is.

**AT HOME** Think of another noun that names a place. Draw a picture of the place.

Name

**NOUNS THAT NAME PLACES** • Say the noun that names each place on this page. • Then circle the kinds of places that were in the poem.

**EXTEND** Change the poem "This Is the Key to the City" to tell where your favorite toy is.

**AT HOME** Name several different places in your house.

Name ______________________________ READ TOGETHER

store

bird

hiker

street

mailbox

runner

skater

airport

giraffe

**NOUNS THAT NAME PLACES** • Say the name of each picture. • Then draw a circle around each place.

**EXTEND** Draw a picture of a place in your neighborhood. Write the name of the place.

**AT HOME** Draw a picture of a place you like to go. Tell about the place you drew.

Name ______________________________

**SEQUENCE** ● ★ Draw a circle around the picture that shows what happened first. ▲ Draw a circle around the picture that shows what happened last.

**EXTEND** Tell a story about two animals. Tell what happens first, next, and last.

**AT HOME** Draw pictures to tell the story of a time you visited somebody. Put the pictures in order.

Name______________________________________________ READ TOGETHER

**SPECIAL NOUNS THAT NAME PLACES, DAYS** Find the name of each place on a sign. • Circle the name. Look at the calendar pages below. • Circle the name of each day of the week.

**EXTEND** Draw a picture of your favorite place. Write the name of the place below your picture.

**AT HOME** Draw a picture of something you did today. Tell about your picture and say what day it is.

Name ______________________________

**SPECIAL NOUNS (DAYS, PLACE NAMES)**
• Draw a picture of your school. • Say the name of your school. • Then say the names of the days of the week when you go to school.

**EXTEND** Make a list of three places that have special names.

**AT HOME** Say the name of your town, your state, and your country.

Name____________________ READ TOGETHER

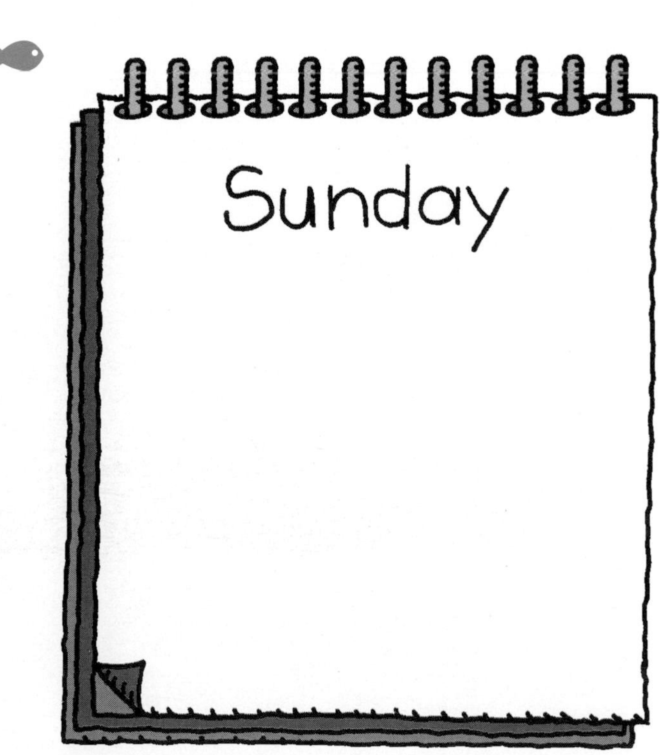


**SPECIAL NOUNS THAT NAME PLACES, DAYS**
Draw a circle around the two names of places in the pictures. Draw a circle around the names of the days of the week. Draw a picture of something you do on each day.

**EXTEND** Draw a special place you have visited. Write its name.

**AT HOME** Look at signs for the names of places near your home.

Name ______________________________ READ TOGETHER

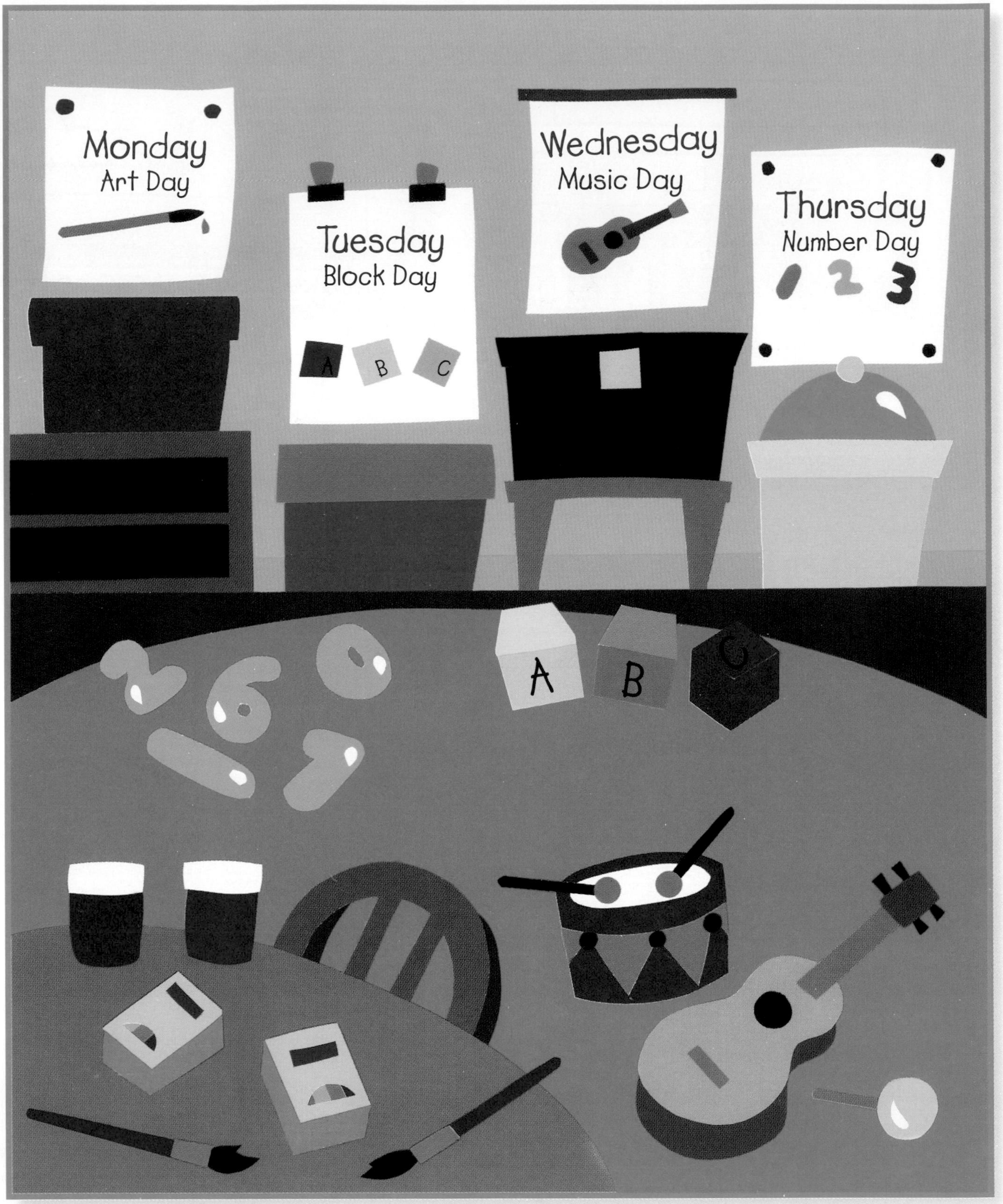

Monday
Art Day

Tuesday
Block Day

Wednesday
Music Day

Thursday
Number Day

**ENVIRONMENTAL PRINT** • Draw a green circle around the items that would be used on Art Day. • Draw a blue circle around the items for Block Day. • Draw a red circle around the items for Music Day. • Draw a purple circle around the items for Number Day.

**EXTEND** Draw a picture to show something you did today. Make a sign that tells what you did.

**AT HOME** Make up a song to tell what your family does each day of the week.

Name

bird

store

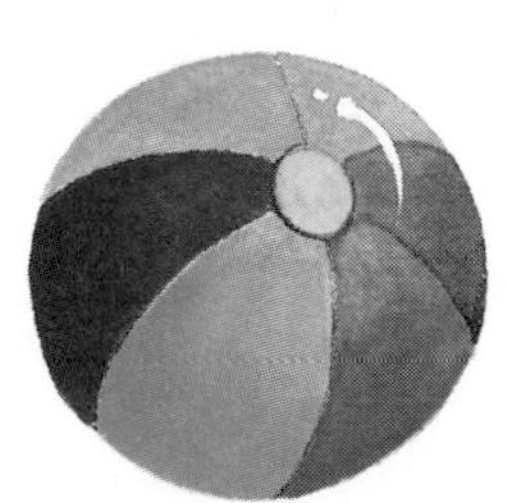
ball

school

horse

tree

boy

skunk

girl

dog

man

crayon

**UNIT 2 WRAP-UP: Review Nouns** • Say the names of the pictures in each row. Draw a circle around the words that name places. Draw a circle around the words that name animals. Draw a circle around the words that name people.

Name

**UNIT 2 WRAP-UP: Draw Pictures and Write**
• Draw a picture of two people who work in your neighborhood. • Write a sentence about each person. • In each sentence, use the noun that tells who the person is.

# Tell Me About It

UNIT 3

Name

**UNIT 3 OPENER** • Think of a building you would like to make with blocks. • Draw a picture of the building and write about it.

Name

**ACTION VERBS** • Draw a red circle around the grandmother and child who read. • Draw a blue circle around the children who pour. • Draw a green circle around the children who build.

**EXTEND** Draw a picture of something you do at home. Write the action verb that tells what you do.

**AT HOME** Think of five things you like to do. Say an action word for each of these things.

Name ____________________

**ACTION VERBS** • Look at the animals in each row and tell what each is doing. • Draw circles around the animals that are doing the same action.

**EXTEND** Make up animal riddles such as: What moos? (a cow) What roars? (a lion)

**AT HOME** Draw pictures of animals doing different actions. Talk about your pictures.

Name ____________________ READ TOGETHER

run

run

read

jump

swim

jump

dig

fly kite

dig

**ACTION VERBS** • Circle the two pictures in each row that show the same action.

**EXTEND** Draw a picture of yourself learning to do something new.

**AT HOME** Draw a picture of yourself doing something you like to do.

Name ____________________ READ TOGETHER

moon

1

2

3

4

sun



**FOLLOW DIRECTIONS** • Draw a path for the moon to visit the sun's palace. • Start at the moon. • Go *right* to star 1. • Go *down* to star 2. • Go *left* to star 3. • Go *down* to star 4 and *right* to the palace. • Draw the sun in the palace.

**EXTEND** Play a game of "Simon Says." Take turns giving and following directions.

**AT HOME** Give someone directions for walking from your bed to the kitchen in your home.

Name

**MORE ACTION VERBS** • Draw a red circle around the child who floats. • Draw a blue circle around the children who run. • Draw a green circle around the child who cycles. • Draw a black circle around the child who climbs.

**EXTEND** Draw a picture of what you do at the playground. Label your picture with an action verb.

**AT HOME** Talk about what the children in the pictures are doing.

Name

**MORE ACTION VERBS** • Draw a circle around the pictures that show what the children do in "Rope Rhyme." • Name the action word that tells what each of these children is doing. • Then talk about the other pictures on the page.

**EXTEND** Draw a picture of yourself playing. Name the action word that tells what you are doing.

**AT HOME** Name some action words that tell what you do at school. Pick one and draw a picture of it.

Name________________________________ READ TOGETHER

saw

dry

wash

hammer

buy

cut

**MORE ACTION VERBS** • Draw a line to connect people who might be helping each other. • Tell what they do.

**EXTEND** Draw a picture of a friend helping you do something.

**AT HOME** Discuss with family members ways you can help each other.

Name ______________________ READ TOGETHER

cottage

barn

pine tree

garden

Granny's cottage

well

tree

**USING A MAP** • How did the boy in the story find the little red house? • Draw a line to show the path he took.

**EXTEND** Act out the story using pictures of the places the boy went. Go from place to place.

**AT HOME** Use the map on this page to help retell the story of "The Little Red House."

Name ____________________

**PAST TENSE VERBS** • Look at the pictures.
• Say the verb that tells what the people did.

**EXTEND** Draw and label a picture of something you did yesterday at school.

**AT HOME** Tell a story about something you did last Saturday.

Name________________________________

**PAST-TENSE VERBS** • Draw a circle around each picture that shows something the bunny did in the poem. • Name the action word that tells what the bunny did in each picture you circled.

**EXTEND** Look at each picture you did not circle. Use an action word to tell what the bunny did.

**AT HOME** Draw a picture to show this sentence: *The bunny painted.*

Name________________________________ READ TOGETHER

cooked

painted

**PAST-TENSE VERBS** • Look at the pictures. • Tell what each person did. • Then draw your own pictures to show *cooked* and *painted*.

**EXTEND** Draw a picture to show something you did yesterday. Write a sentence to tell about it.

**AT HOME** Draw a picture to show something you did at school today. Tell someone at home about it.

Name

**REALITY/FANTASY** • Draw a circle around the picture in each row that shows something that could really happen. • Draw a line under the picture in each row that shows something make-believe.

**EXTEND** Draw pictures of an animal doing something real and something make-believe.

**AT HOME** Draw a picture that shows something make-believe. Tell about your picture.

Name

***IS, ARE, WAS, WERE*** • Draw a red circle around the woman who *is* raking. • Draw a blue circle around the woman who *was* raking. • Draw a green circle around the apples that *are* on the tree. • Draw a black circle around the apples that *were* picked.

**EXTEND** Look at one of the pictures. Tell a story about it to a partner.

**AT HOME** Draw a picture of a tree. Tell how to finish this sentence: The tree is ______________.

Name

***IS, ARE, WAS, WERE*** Say a sentence about the picture using *is*. Say a sentence about the picture using *are*. Say a sentence about the picture using *was*. Say a sentence about the picture using *were*.

**EXTEND** Talk about the mice in the story. Use the verbs *is*, *are*, *was*, and *were*.

**AT HOME** Use the pictures on the page to tell your own story about some mice.

Name ______________________________ READ TOGETHER

# The dog is big.

# The flowers are red.

# The kittens were sleeping.

***IS, ARE, WAS, WERE*** • Listen to the sentence. • Draw a circle around the picture that matches the sentence. • Then think of a sentence for *was.* • Tell your sentence to a partner.

**EXTEND** Make up your own sentences using *is*, *are*, *was* and *were*.

**AT HOME** Make up other sentences about the pictures on this page.

Name________________________________________

**REALITY/FANTASY** • Draw a picture that shows what you think the Tweet in the poem might look like. • Tell if Tweet is real or make-believe, and explain why.

**EXTEND** What might the Tweet's house look like? Draw a picture.

**AT HOME** Tell a family member or friend about the Tweet.

Name ____________________

**WORKING WITH VERBS** • Draw a red circle around the children who clap. • Draw a blue circle around the people who dance. • Draw a green circle around the children who march.

**EXTEND** Write a sentence about one of the pictures.

**AT HOME** Draw a picture of yourself playing in a band. Tell what you do.

Name ______________________________

**WORKING WITH VERBS** • Think about the story "How Animals Talk." • Look at each picture. • Say a sentence that tells what the animal in each picture is doing.

**EXTEND** Draw and label pictures of your favorite animals. Tell how the animals talk.

**AT HOME** Name some animals in your neighborhood. Tell how these animals talk.

Name________________________________ READ TOGETHER

jump

ride

skate

toss

**WORKING WITH VERBS** • Put a red circle around the child who rides. • Put a blue circle around the children who skate. • Put a green circle around the child who jumps. • Put a black circle around the children who toss the ball.

**EXTEND** Draw a picture of yourself playing your favorite sport. Write a sentence about the picture.

**AT HOME** Draw a picture of someone you know playing a sport. Tell about your picture.

Name

**REALITY/FANTASY** • In each row, draw a circle around the picture that shows something make-believe. • Draw a line under the picture that something real.

**EXTEND** Find a book in the library about real wolves and a book with a make-believe wolf.

**AT HOME** Tell your family the story of "Groundhog's Dance."

Name________________________________

**UNIT 3 WRAP-UP: Review Verbs** • Use an action verb to tell what is happening in each picture. • Then use the word *is* or *are* to tell where the dog or dogs are in the picture.

Name

**UNIT 3 WRAP-UP: Write About the Picture**
• Imagine that you are at this puppet show. • Write what you think will happen. • Try to use action verbs.

# What's New?

UNIT 4

Name

**UNIT 4 OPENER** • Draw a picture of what you might see on a nature trail. • Write about the picture.

Name________________________________________

1.

2.

3.

4.

**WHAT IS A SENTENCE?** • Say a sentence about each picture.

**EXTEND** Think of a wild animal. Write a sentence about it.

**AT HOME** Draw a picture of a bird. Use sentences to tell about your picture.

Name

**WHAT IS A SENTENCE?** • Draw a circle around the picture that shows something the mice did in the story. Then tell what is happening in each picture you circled.

**EXTEND** Draw a picture of something else a mouse does. Tell a sentence about it.

**AT HOME** List all the things you have learned about mice.

Name

READ TOGETHER

1.

Ben walks in the rain.

2.

Anna

**WHAT IS A SENTENCE?** • *1.* Look at the picture and listen to the sentence. *2.* Look at the picture and complete the sentence or have your teacher help you complete it.

**EXTEND** Draw a picture. Make up a sentence about your drawing.

**AT HOME** Ask someone to read the sentence about the boy. Make up another sentence about him.

Name ____________________ READ TOGETHER

1.

goose

Ee

2.

egg

Ll

3.

lake

Gg



**REFERENCE SOURCES** • Look at the pictures and words. • Where would you find each picture in a picture dictionary? • Match the picture to the same letter on the right that the word begins with. • Then write the word on the line.

**EXTEND** Use a real picture dictionary to find the names of other animals and plants.

**AT HOME** Draw pictures of two things whose names begin with the same letter.

Name

1.

2.

3.

4.

**TELLING SENTENCES** • Make up a telling sentence about each picture.

**EXTEND** Draw a picture of your favorite toy or game. Write a sentence that tells about it.

**AT HOME** Tell a story about a place you like to visit.

Name________________________________________

1.

2.

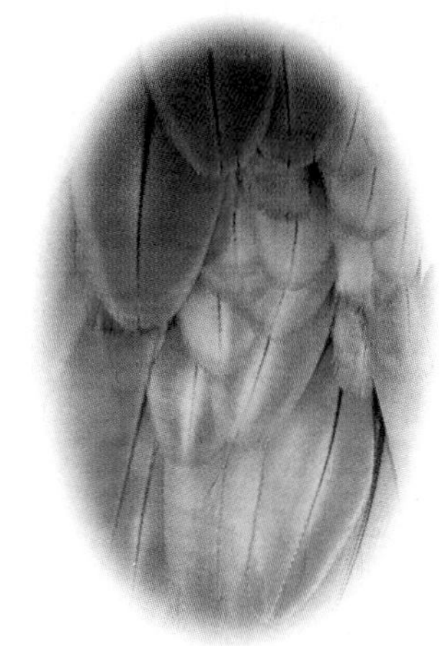

3.

**TELLING SENTENCES** • Look at the animal in each row. • Then draw a circle around the picture that shows what it needs to stay warm. • Say a sentence about the animal.

**EXTEND** Draw a picture of something you wear to keep warm. Tell a sentence about it.

**AT HOME** Say a few sentences about how animals keep warm in winter.

Name________________________________ READ TOGETHER

1.

The bears play.

2.

The bears

**TELLING SENTENCES** • *1.* Look at the picture and listen to the sentence. • *2.* Look at the picture and complete the sentence or have your teacher help you complete it.

**EXTEND** Make up a story about bear cubs.

**AT HOME** Make up other sentences about the pictures on this page.

Name ____________________

1.

2.

3.

**MAIN IDEA** • Which picture in each row shows something Crinkleroot would like to see? Draw a circle around the picture.

**EXTEND** Draw a picture of a place that Crinkleroot would like to visit.

**AT HOME** Go outdoors with a family member to find things that Crinkleroot would like.

Name

1.

2.

**ASKING SENTENCES** • Make up an asking sentence for each picture.

**EXTEND** Write an asking sentence about one of the pictures. Ask a partner to answer it.

**AT HOME** Find pictures in magazines and ask questions about them.

Name ____________________

1.

2.

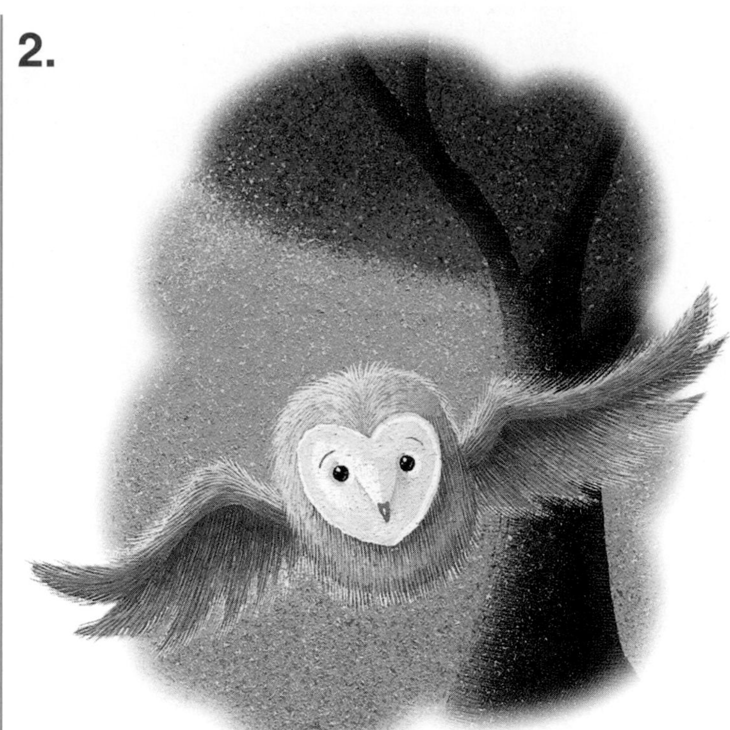

3.

4.

**ASKING SENTENCES** • What is happening in each picture? • Think of a question to ask about the picture.

**EXTEND** Draw a picture of an animal. Have a classmate ask a question about your picture.

**AT HOME** Ask someone at home: What is your favorite animal? Draw the animal.

Name

READ TOGETHER

1. What is a fish?

2. What is a cat?

3. What is a ?

**ASKING SENTENCES** • *1, 2.* Listen to the questions. • Circle the picture that answers each question. • *3.* Finish the question by writing an animal's name or have your teacher help you write it. • Draw a picture of the animal.

**EXTEND** Draw a picture of a person. Write an asking sentence about the person.

**AT HOME** Take turns making up asking sentences about pictures you find in magazines and books.

Name

READ TOGETHER

1. What are star cookies?

2. What is a shooting star?

3. What is an airplane?

**ASK QUESTIONS** • Listen to your teacher read each question. • Draw a circle around the picture that answers the question.

**EXTEND** Draw a picture of something you would like to learn about. Write a question about it.

**AT HOME** Ask an adult some questions about what he or she did as a child.

Name

1.

2.

3.

4.

**EXCLAIMING SENTENCES** • Draw a circle around the picture that goes with each sentence. • Red circle: "The fireworks are pretty!" • Blue circle: "There's a whale!" • Green circle: "It's a windy day!" • Make up an exclaiming sentence about the rainbow.

**EXTEND** Think of an animal you would be excited to see. Write an exclaiming sentence about it.

**AT HOME** Tell a story about each picture on this page. Use exclaiming sentences.

Name ______________________________

1.

2.

3.

**EXCLAIMING SENTENCES** • *1-2.* Say an exclaiming sentence for each picture. • *3.* Then draw a picture of a time when you were happy. • Say an exclaiming sentence to go with it.

**EXTEND** Draw a picture of an exciting surprise. Make up a sentence to go with it.

**AT HOME** Say an exclaiming sentence that tells something exciting about an animal.

Name ______________________________ READ TOGETHER

1. It's your birthday!

2. This is a surprise!

3. I love hats!

**EXCLAIMING SENTENCES** • Listen to the sentence. • Draw a circle around the picture that matches the sentence.

**EXTEND** Draw a circle around the mark at the end of each sentence. Tell a story about the pictures.

**AT HOME** Draw a picture of something that would surprise you.

Name________________________________________ READ TOGETHER

1. The boy cried "Wolf!"

2. The people ran to help.

3. The wolf really came.

**MAIN IDEA** • Listen to your teacher read each sentence. • Draw a circle around the picture that goes with the sentence.

**EXTEND** Using one sentence, explain what lesson the shepherd boy in the story learned.

**AT HOME** Use the circled pictures on this page to help you tell the story to a friend.

Name

1.

2.

3.

**SUBJECT/VERB AGREEMENT** • Say a sentence about each picture.

**EXTEND** Draw a picture of the beach. Write a sentence about your picture.

**AT HOME** Use sentences to talk about each picture on this page.

Name________________________________

1.

2.

3.

**SUBJECT/VERB AGREEMENT** • Say a sentence to tell what is happening in each picture. • Then draw a circle around the picture in each row that shows something that happened in the story.

**EXTEND** Draw a picture of your favorite part of the story. Say a sentence to tell about your picture.

**AT HOME** Tell someone at home a few sentences about the story.

Name

The pup chases the duck.

The pups chase the duck.

2.

**SUBJECT/VERB AGREEMENT** • *1.* Listen to each sentence. • Draw a line under the sentence that tells what is happening in the picture. • *2.* Look at the picture. • Write a sentence to tell about the picture or have your teacher help you write a sentence.

**EXTEND** Draw a picture of two animals. Make up sentences about your picture.

**AT HOME** Tell a story about the pictures on this page.

Name___________________________________________

**1.**

---

**2.**

---

**3.**

---

**MAIN IDEA** • In each row, there is a picture that shows something important from the poem. • Draw a circle around the picture. • Say one sentence that tells about each of the three pictures you circled.

**EXTEND** Write a sentence that tells what corn seeds need in order to grow.

**AT HOME** Use the circled pictures on this page to tell how corn seeds grow.

Name

1.

2.

3.

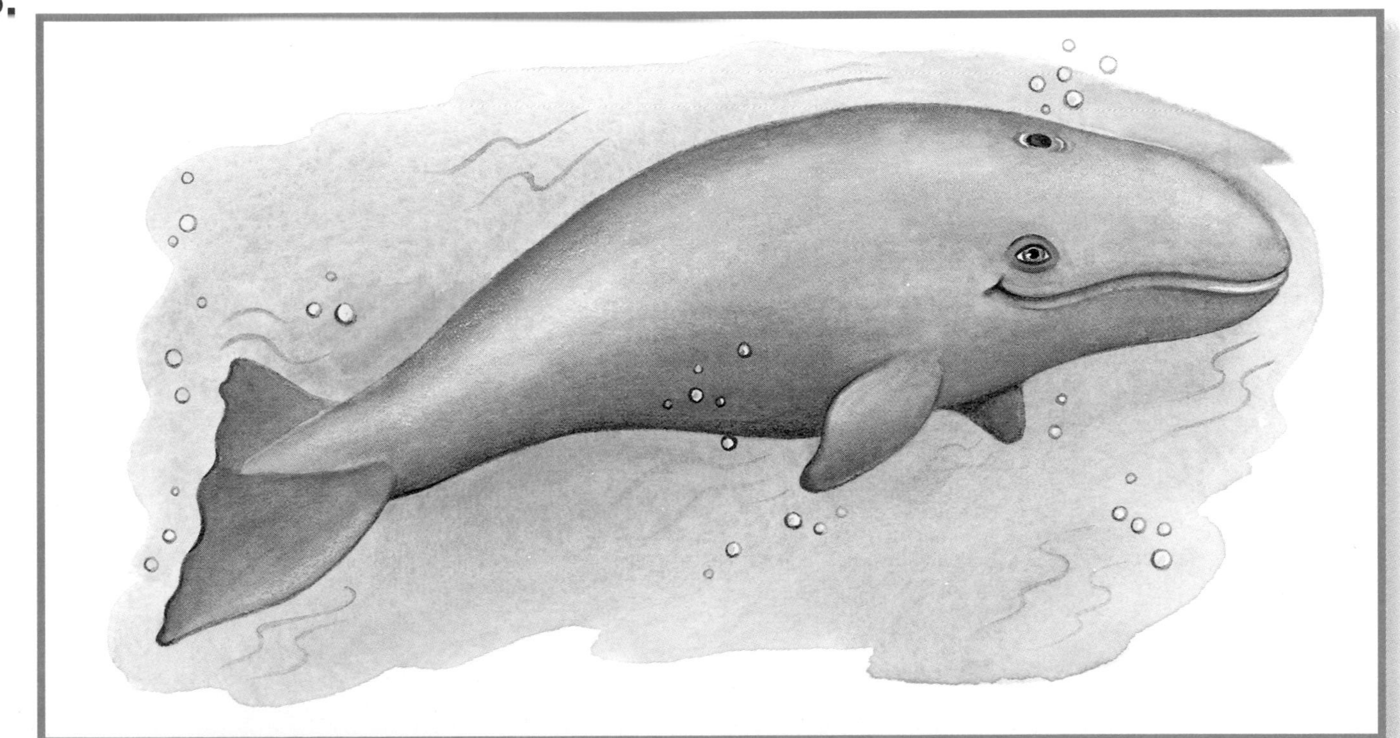

**UNIT 4 WRAP-UP: Review Sentences** • Look at the pictures. *1.* Say a telling sentence. *2.* Say an asking sentence. *3.* Say an exclaiming sentence.

Name

**UNIT 4 WRAP-UP: Write About the Picture**
• Write a telling sentence about what is happening in the picture. • Then write an asking sentence and an exclaiming sentence about the picture.

# Put On Your Thinking Cap

UNIT 5

Name

**UNIT 5 OPENER** • Draw a picture of you and a friend fixing something. • Write about your picture.

Name ______________________________

I.

2.

**COLOR WORDS** • *1.* Name the color of each child's shirt. • Then draw a circle around each child's shirt using the same color crayon. *2.* Draw a picture using your favorite color. Write a label naming the color.

**EXTEND** Draw a picture of two kites. Write a label that tells about the color of each kite.

**AT HOME** Imagine a kite you would like. Talk about all the colors it would be.

Name________________________________ READ TOGETHER

1.

2.

3.

**CHART** • One bird in each row of the chart has no color. • Use the rest of the row to decide what color the bird should be. • Color the bird.

**EXTEND** Think of other things that are the same three colors as the birds.

**AT HOME** Look for birds outside. Count how many you see that have bright-colored feathers.

Name ______________________

1.

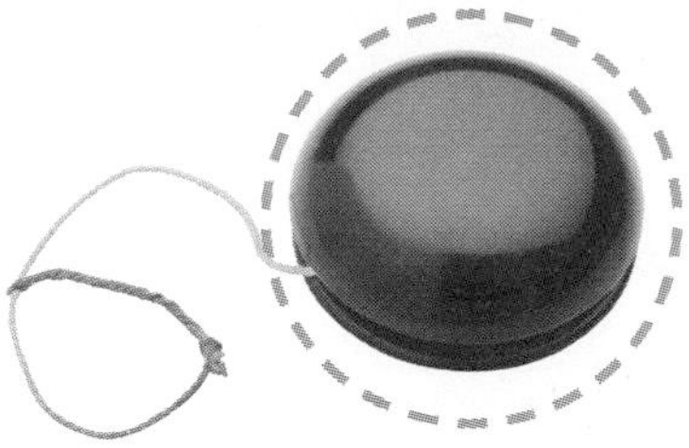

2.

3.

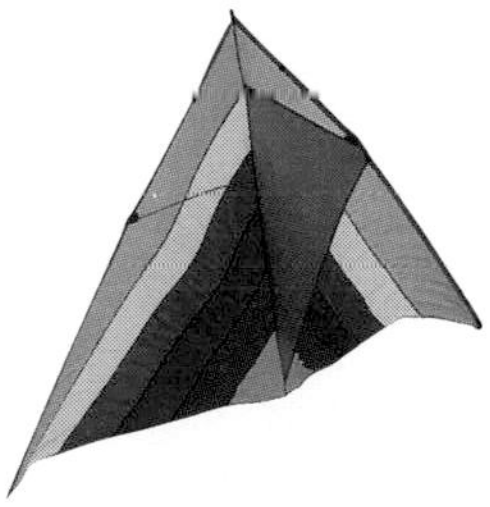

4.

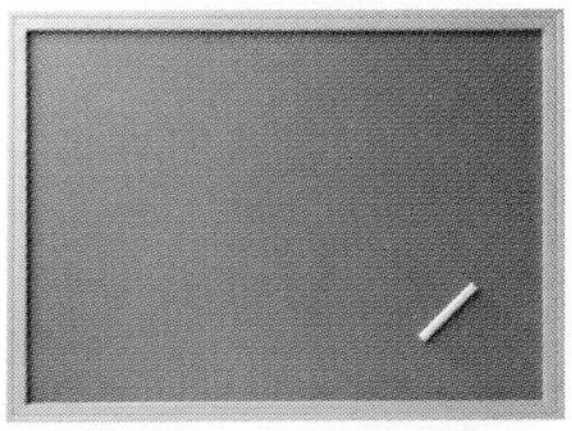

**SIZE, SHAPE, AND NUMBER WORDS** • Name the shape. • Look for the same shape in each row. • Trace each one you find. • Tell how many you find.

**EXTEND** Use the shapes to make a picture. Count how many of each kind of shape you used.

**AT HOME** Look for the shapes at home. Talk about the things that have each shape.

Name ___________________________________________

1.

2.

3.

**SIZE, SHAPE, AND NUMBER WORDS** • Look at the pictures in each row. • *1*. Draw a circle around the pictures of big dogs. • *2*. Draw a circle around the pictures of thin dogs. • *3*. Draw a circle around the picture that shows three dogs.

**EXTEND** Use size, shape, and number words to describe the dogs you did not circle.

**AT HOME** Draw two dogs. Use size and shape words to describe them.

Name________________________________________ READ TOGETHER

1.

six rectangles

2.

two circles

3.

four triangles

4.

little squares

**SIZE, SHAPE, AND NUMBER WORDS** • *1-3.* Look at the pictures. • Listen as your teacher reads the words below each picture. • Trace the shapes in each picture the words tell about. • *4.* Trace around each side of the game.

**EXTEND** Draw a picture that contains shapes. Use shape and number words to describe your picture.

**AT HOME** Look at the building you live in. Use size, shape and number words to tell what you see.

Name________________________________________ READ TOGETHER

1.

soft fur

red feathers

2.

pink ears

chubby cheeks

3.

sings

squeaks

4.

whiskered face

green shell



**DETAILS** • Look at each picture. • Listen to the two words or phrases below each picture. • Draw a circle around the words that tell about the hamster in the poem.

**EXTEND** Draw a picture of the hamster described in the story. Write a sentence about it.

**AT HOME** Think about dogs and hamsters. List ways they are different and ways they are the same.

Name ____________________

1.

2.

3.

**SENSE WORDS** • Name the sense that each child is using. • Draw a circle around one more thing that lets you use that sense. • Think of a word that tells how each thing you circled sounds, tastes, or smells.

**EXTEND** Draw pictures of things you see, hear, and taste. Write a sense word for each one.

**AT HOME** Use different words to tell about how things look, sound, taste, smell, and feel.

Name

1.

2.

3.

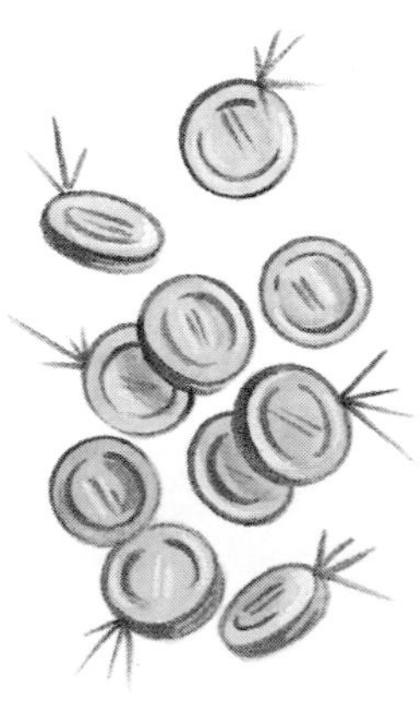

**STORY DETAILS** • Think about the story "Theft of a Smell." • Draw a circle around the answer to each question. • *1.* What did the neighbor enjoy smelling? • *2.* Which person did the baker speak to about his neighbor? • *3.* What did the baker enjoy hearing?

**EXTEND** Draw something you enjoy smelling. Then draw something else you enjoy hearing.

**AT HOME** Draw pictures of three foods whose smells you like most.

Name ________________________________

**1.**

**2.**

**3.**

**FEELING WORDS** • How does the first picture in each row make you feel? • Circle the picture at the right that shows how you feel.

**EXTEND** Draw pictures of different things that make you feel happy, sad, or surprised.

**AT HOME** Look at pictures of people in magazines. Talk about how you think the people feel.

Name______________________________

1.

2.

3.

**FEELING WORDS** • The pictures on the left show something that happened in the story. • The pictures on the right show how Carl felt about each thing that happened. • Draw lines to match the pictures.

**EXTEND** Make a list of three things that make you feel smart.

**AT HOME** Draw two friends at school. Then tell how you think they might feel.

Name ______________________ READ TOGETHER

1.

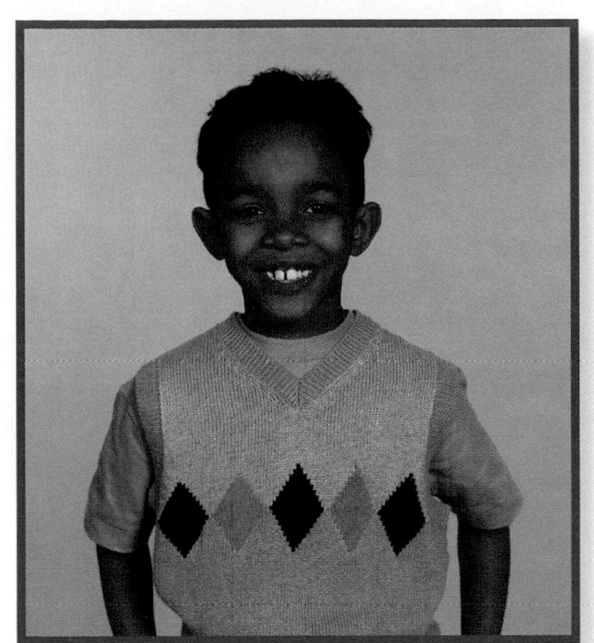

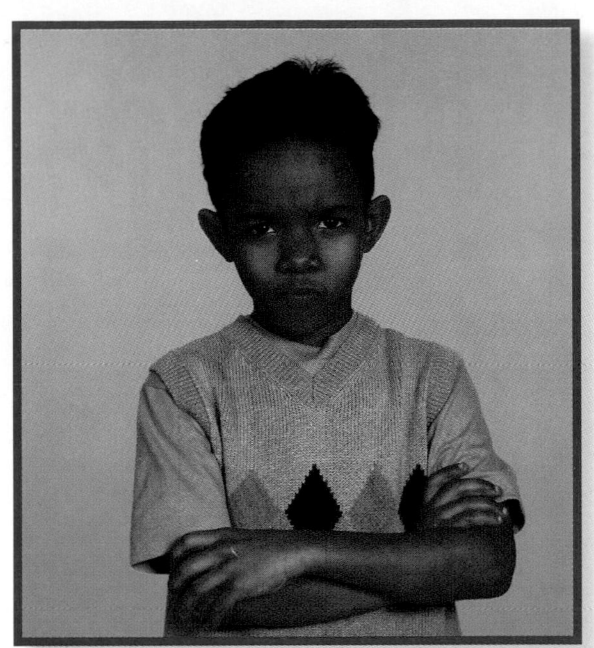

# Sam is happy.

2.

**FEELING WORDS** • *1.* Look at the pictures and listen to the sentence. • Draw a circle around the picture that goes with the sentence. • *2.* Write a sentence about how someone feels or have your teacher help you write it. • Draw a picture to go with your sentence.

**EXTEND** Draw someone whose face shows feeling. Write a sentence that tells how the person feels.

**AT HOME** Think of a word that describes a feeling. Ask someone to make a face that shows that feeling.

Name ______________________________

1.

2.

3.

**STORY DETAILS** • *1.* Draw a circle around what the good woodcutter saw. • *2.* Draw a circle around how the good woodcutter felt when the coins fell from the tree. • *3.* Draw a circle around the good woodcutter.

**EXTEND** Think of what lesson the bad woodcutter learned. Tell about the lesson.

**AT HOME** Tell someone what happened to the bad woodcutter.

Name

1.

2.

3.

**WORDS THAT COMPARE** • *1*. Draw a circle around the tallest block building. • *2*. Draw a circle around the smallest bike. • *3*. Draw a circle around the longest fish.

**EXTEND** Draw three pictures to illustrate the words *small*, *smaller*, and *smallest*.

**AT HOME** Find things in your home that are *big*, *bigger*, and *biggest*.

Name

1.

2.

**COMPARING** • *1*. Draw a circle around the *longest* snake. • *2*. Draw a circle around the *tallest* tree.

**EXTEND** With a partner, find things around your school that are longer than a pencil.

**AT HOME** Use clay or paper to make three snakes that are *small*, *smaller*, and *smallest*.

Name____________________ READ TOGETHER

1. This house is wider.

2. This car is smaller.

3. This tree is the biggest.

**WORDS THAT COMPARE** • Listen to the sentence. • Draw a circle around the part of the picture the sentence tells about.

**EXTEND** Draw pictures of three pets that are *big*, *bigger*, and *biggest*.

**AT HOME** Compare your family's shoes. Arrange them from biggest to smallest.

Name ____________________ READ TOGETHER

1.

horns

eyes

hooves

ears

tail

legs

2.

eyes

nose

whiskers

ears

tail

feet



**DIAGRAMS** • On the first diagram, draw a line from each label to the correct body part on the goat. • On the second diagram, draw a line from each label to the correct body part on the rabbit.

**EXTEND** Draw a picture of your favorite animal. Label the animal's body parts.

**AT HOME** Draw a picture of an elephant. Tell where the eyes, ears, trunk, and feet are.

Name________________________________

1.

The two green balls are big.

---

2.

The red chair is soft.

---

**UNIT 5 WRAP-UP: Review Describing Words**
• Look at the pictures. • Listen to each sentence.
• Draw a circle around the picture that the sentence tells about.

Name

**UNIT 5 WRAP-UP: Write About the Picture**
• Name the shapes you see in the mobile. How many of each can you count? • How do the children feel?
• Use describing words to tell about the picture.

# Pick a Plan

UNIT 6

Name

**UNIT 6 OPENER** • Draw a picture of a garden you would like to plant. • Write the names of some things that are in your garden.

Name ______________________________

1.

2.

3.

4.

**PRONOUNS *I, YOU*** • Look at the activities shown in the pictures. • Draw a circle around the activity you would choose. • Ask a partner "What did you choose?" • Tell your partner what you chose.

**EXTEND** Draw a picture of yourself having fun. Use the word *I* to write a sentence about it.

**AT HOME** Draw a picture of yourself playing outside. Use the word *I* to tell about it.

Name ______________________________

1.

2.

3.

**STORY STRUCTURE** • Draw a circle around the picture that shows what happened at the beginning of the story. • Draw a line under the picture that shows what happened in the middle of the story. • Draw two lines to show what happened at the end of the story.

**EXTEND** Draw pictures that show the beginning, middle, and end of another story.

**AT HOME** Use these pictures to tell the beginning, middle, and end of the story.

Name

1.

2.

**PRONOUNS *HE, SHE, IT*** • Draw a line from each person to the picture that shows the book that person chose. • Use the words *he*, *she*, and *it* to tell about what each person chose.

**EXTEND** Draw a picture of a girl and a boy. Use the words *he* and *she* to write about the picture.

**AT HOME** Take a book home from the library. Talk about the pictures in the book.

Name

1.

2.

3.

**PRONOUNS *HE, SHE, IT*** • Circle the picture that goes with each sentence. • *1. He is a pet dog.* • *2. It is a kitten.* • *3. She is the mother cat.*

**EXTEND** Draw two pets that you know. Use the pronouns *he*, *she*, and *it* to tell about them.

**AT HOME** Draw the cat, dog, and a kitten from the poem. Label each picture *he*, *she*, or *it.*

Name



1.

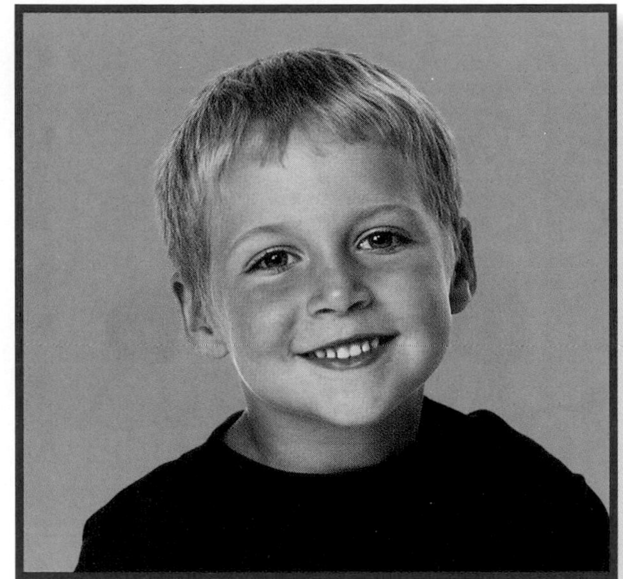

he she it

2.

he she it

3.

4.

**PRONOUNS *HE, SHE, IT*** • *1, 2.* Look at the person or thing in each picture. • Choose the pronoun that goes with the picture. • *3, 4.* Write *he*, *she* or *it* on the line to match each picture.

**EXTEND** Draw a picture of a person. Write a sentence about the person using the word *he* or *she*.

**AT HOME** Cut out pictures from magazines. Use *he*, *she* and *it* to tell about the pictures.

Name

1\.

2\.

3\.

4\.

**STORY STRUCTURE** • Draw a circle around the picture that shows how the tree looked at the beginning and end of the story. • Tell what happened in the middle of the story.

**EXTEND** Draw three pictures that show a beginning, middle, and end to the story.

**AT HOME** Use the pictures on this page to help you retell the story of the little tree.

Name ______________________________

**PRONOUNS *WE, THEY*** • Draw a picture of something you and your friends might choose to do on the playground. • Use the pronouns *we* and *they* to talk about your picture.

**EXTEND** Write a sentence about something fun you do with a friend. Use the word *we*.

**AT HOME** Talk about a game you play with friends. Use the words *we* and *they*.

Name ______________________________________ READ TOGETHER

1. Beginning

2. Middle

3. End

**STORY STRUCTURE** • Listen as your teacher reads the labels for each picture. • Then draw a picture that shows what was on top of the mountain at the beginning, the middle, and the end of the story.

**EXTEND** With three other people, act out the beginning, middle, and end of this story.

**AT HOME** Tell what happened in the middle part of this story.

Name

1.

2.

3.

**PRONOUNS AND VERBS** • Draw a circle around the two pictures in each row that can be described using the same pronoun. • Say a sentence for each picture in the row.

**EXTEND** Draw a picture of a friend. Use the words *he* or *she* to write about the picture.

**AT HOME** Draw a picture of two animals playing. Use the word *they* to talk about the picture.

Name

1.

2.

3.

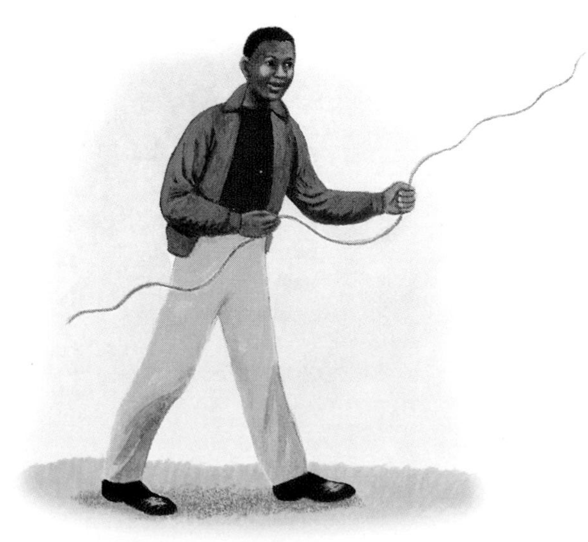



**PRONOUN/VERB AGREEMENT** • Circle the picture that goes with each sentence. • *1. It flies.* • *2. They run.* • *3. He holds the string.* • Make up sentences using *they* and *she* to tell about the girl and her dad.

**EXTEND** Draw a picture of some classmates. Use the pronouns *he*, *she*, and *they* to tell about it.

**AT HOME** Make up riddles about family members. Use the pronouns *he*, *she*, and *they*.

Name______________________________ READ TOGETHER

1.

She feeds her fish.

2.

**PRONOUNS AND VERBS** • *1.* Draw a circle around the pronoun *she* in the sentence. • *2.* Draw a picture of yourself doing something. • Write about your picture or have your teacher help you write about it. • Use the word *I*.

**EXTEND** Draw a picture of a family member. Use *he* or *she* to write a sentence about the person.

**AT HOME** Use *I* to tell about something you did at school with a friend.

Name

1.

2.

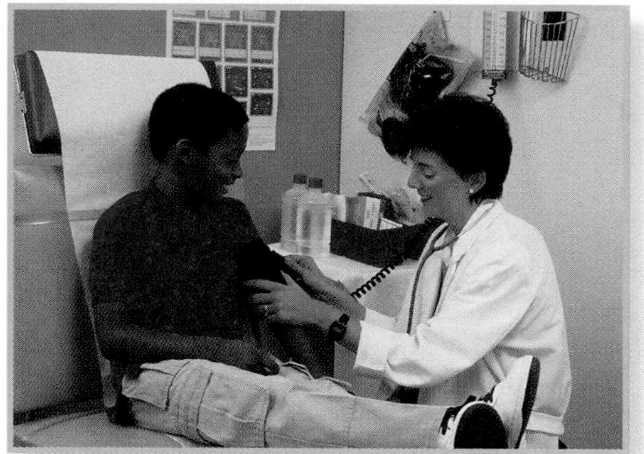

3.



**USING THE LIBRARY** • *1, 2.* Draw a circle around the picture in each row that shows something that Tyler does at the library. • *3.* Write about something else Tyler does at the library or have your teacher help you write.

**EXTEND** Draw a picture of something you like to do at the library. Write a sentence about your picture.

**AT HOME** Tell someone about the things Tyler saw at the library.

Name

1.

2.

3.

**WORKING WITH PRONOUNS** • *1, 2.* Say what the boy and girl chose for lunch. • *3.* Then draw a picture showing what you would choose. • Use pronouns to tell how the three lunches are alike and different.

**EXTEND** Draw a picture of a breakfast meal. Use the words *I* and *it* to write about your picture.

**AT HOME** Draw the favorite foods of people you know. Use pronouns to talk about the picture.

Name______________________________

1.

2.

3.

**WORKING WITH PRONOUNS** • Draw a circle around the picture that goes with each sentence. • *1. I am a little brother.* • *2. She is my sister.* • *3. They are our parents.* • Then point to each picture and say the pronoun *he*, *she*, or *they* that goes with it.

**EXTEND** Draw pictures of another family. Label your pictures. For example: *He is the dad.*

**AT HOME** Draw a baby picture of yourself. Use the pronoun *I* to talk about your picture.

Name ____________________ READ TOGETHER

1.

She We

____________ plants.

2.

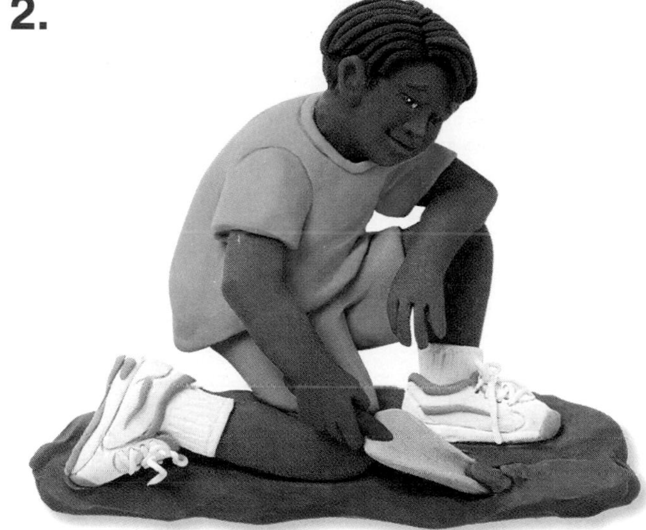

She He

____________ digs.

3.

It She

____________ grows.

**WORKING WITH PRONOUNS** • Draw a circle around the pronoun that matches each picture. • Write the pronoun on the line to complete the sentence.

**EXTEND** Draw a picture of a friend. Write *he* or *she* under it.

**AT HOME** Draw a picture of a person from a book. Label it with *he* or *she*.

Name ______________________ READ TOGETHER

1.

2.

**ALPHABETICAL ORDER** • Look at the letters in each bowl of soup. • In each bowl, say the names of the first two letters that are marked. • Then, draw a line to the letter that comes next in the alphabet. • Keep going until you reach the last letter.

**EXTEND** On a new line for each bowl, write out the letters in the order you put them.

**AT HOME** Find cans of soup at home. Put the letters from the labels in alphabetical order.

Name________________________________

Review

READ TOGETHER

1.

__________ buys tickets.

He She

2.

__________ takes tickets.

It She

3.

__________ is fun.

We It

**UNIT 6 WRAP-UP: Review Pronouns** • Listen to each sentence. • Circle the pronoun below that belongs in the sentence. • On the line, write the pronoun that belongs in the sentence.

Name



Dear

From



**UNIT 6 WRAP-UP: Write a Letter** • Write a letter to a friend. • Tell about a fun time you had with your family or another friend. • Try to use the words *I*, *you*, and *we* in your letter.

# Picture Dictionary

## Aa

airplane

ant

apple

## Bb

bear

boat

bus

# Picture Dictionary

## Cc

**c**ook

**c**orn

**c**ow

## Dd

**d**ance

**d**inosaur

**d**oor

# Picture Dictionary

**e**at

**e**gg

**e**lephant

**f**arm

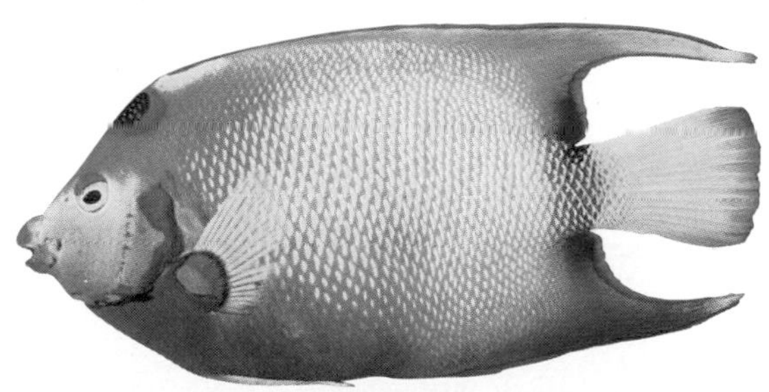

**f**ish

**f**lower

# Picture Dictionary

## Gg

gate

giraffe

goat

## Hh

happy

hat

hop

# Picture Dictionary

ice

igloo

insect

jeans

juice

jump

# Picture Dictionary

**k**ey

**k**ick

**k**ite

**l**adder

**l**eaf

Dear Bill,
Thank you for coming
to my birthday party.
I really like the book
you gave me. You are
a great friend.
Sincerely,
Lena

**l**etter

# Picture Dictionary

milk

mix

moon

necklace

nest

nurse

# Picture Dictionary

ocean

octopus

orange

paint

piano

pig

# Picture Dictionary

quarter

queen

quilt

## Rr

rabbit

rainbow

r

# Picture Dictionary

## Ss

shell

sign

swim

## Tt

tent

tiger

tree

# Picture Dictionary

## Uu

umbrella

van

volcano

## Ww

wagon

web

whale

# Picture Dictionary

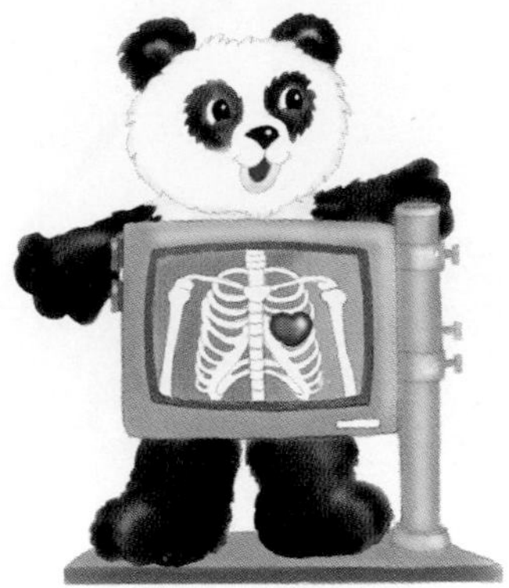

Xray

yard

yo-yo

zebra

zero

zipper

Name ____________________

# My Word List

**MY WORD LIST** • Have your teacher help you make a list of words you have learned.

Name ______________________________

# My Word List

**MY WORD LIST** • Have your teacher help you make a list of words you have learned.

Name ____________________

# My Word List

**MY WORD LIST** • Have your teacher help you make a list of words you have learned.

Name

# My Word List

**MY WORD LIST** • Have your teacher help you make a list of words you have learned.

Name

# My Story

**MY STORY** • Write a story using some of the new words you have learned. • Draw pictures to go with you story.

Name

# My Story

**MY STORY** • Write a story using some of the new words you have learned. • Draw pictures to go with you story.

## ACKNOWLEDGMENTS

**Cover Design and Illustration:** Robert Brook Allen

**Cover Puppet:** Linda Carbone

ILLUSTRATION CREDITS: Winky Adam: 44, 46. Angela Adams: 6, 112. Bernard Adnet: 93. Laurie Anzalone: 118. 148, 153. Martha Avelez: 90. Susan Banta: 60,134. Karen Bell: 47, 48, 95, 96, 102, 110, 154. Joe Boddy: 34, 42, 92. Ken Bowser: 9, 43, 45, 117, 131. Georgia Cawley: 23, 24, 111, 141. Mary Collier: 116. Liz Conrad: 52, 88. Diana Craft: 20, 86, 111, 142, 149, 151, 152,153, 155, 156. Lynn Cravath: 32. Daniel Delvalle: 22. Eldon Doty: 89,126. Kathi Ember: 128. Dorris Ettinger: 124. Dagmar Fehlan: 84. Teresa Flavin: 136. Dave Garbot: 1, 2, 23, 25, 26, 47, 49, 50, 71, 73, 74, 95, 97, 98, 119, 121, 122, 143. Leanor Glynn: 58. Jui Ishida: 10. Cathy Johnson: 56. Erika LeBarre: 36, 100. Pam Levey: 64. Lynn Martin: 8. Margie Moore: 132. Kathleen O'Malley: 70. Bob Pepper: 71, 72. Daniel Power: 114. Victoria Raymond: 130. Mike Reed: 62, 140. Bart Rivers: 40, 54. Bob Shein: 18. Stacey Shuett: 28. Peggy Tagel: 105. Terry Taylor: 66. Consuelo Udave: 76. Amy Vansguard: 94. Sally Vitsky: 39. Elizabeth Wolf: 30, 125, 143.

All photographs are by McGraw-Hill School Division (MHSD) except as noted below.

PHOTO CREDITS: 4 b.l. quad, b. Tim Davis/Tony Stone Images. 4 b.l. quad, r. Maslowski/Visuals Unlimited. 4 b.l. quad, t. Maslowski/Visuals Unlimited. 4 b.r. quad, b. Tom J. Ulrich/Visuals Unlimited. 4 b.r. quad, r. Joe McDonald/AnimalsAnimals. 4 b.r. quad, t. Tom J. Ulrich/Visuals Unlimited. 4 t.l. quad, b. Mary M Steinbacher/Photo Edit. 4 t.l. quad, l. Mary M Steinbacher/Photo Edit. 4 t.l. quad, r. Superstock. 4 t.r. quad, b.l. E.R.Degginger/Animals Animals. 4 t.r. quad, b.r. E.R.Degginger/Animals Animals. 4 t.r.quad, t.l. Glenn Oliver/Visuals Unlimited. 5 bottom row, c.l. Ken Coleman/Photo Edit. 5 bottom row, c.r. Ken Coleman/Photo Edit. 5 bottom row, r. Ken Coleman/Photo Edit. 5 middle row, c.l. Mary Kate Denny/Photo Edit. 5 middle row, c.r. Mary Kate Denny/Photo Edit. 5 middle row, l. Mary Kate Denny/Photo Edit. 005 middle row, r. Mary Kate Denny/Photo Edit. 5 top row, c.l. Ken Coleman/Photo Edit. 5 top row, c.r. Michael Newman/Photo Edit. 5 top row, l. Ken Coleman/Photo Edit. 5 top row, r. Ken Coleman/Photo Edit. 12 b.l. Mitch Reardon/Photo Researchers, Inc. 12 m.l. Art Wolfe/Photo Researchers, Inc. 12 m.r. Frank Oberla/Tony Stone Images. 12 row 3, r. J. & B. Photographers/AnimalsAnimals. 12 t.r. Kevin Schafer/Tony Stone Images. 12 t.r. Leonard Lee Rue/Photo Researchers. 14 row 1, l. John W. Warden/Stock Connection/Picture Quest. 14 row 1, r. Index Stock. 14 row 2, l. Ralph A. Reinhold/ Animals Animals. 14 row 3, l. Index Stock Photography. 14 row 3, r. Robert Maier/Animals Animals. 15 bottom, left Grantpix/Photo Edit. 15 bottom, right Photo Edit. 15 middle, left David Young-Wolff. 15 top, left Bubbles/Petit Format. 15 top, right Superstock. 17 bottom, left Tony Freeman/PhotoEdit. 17 bottom, right Earl Young/FPG. 17 middle, left Dave Bartruff/Stock Boston. 17 middle, right Tom Bean/The Stock Market. 17 top, left Mark Richards/PhotoEdit. 17 top, right David R.Frazier Photolibrary/Photo Researchers,Inc. 21 bottom row, right Superstock. 21 middle row, far left Michael Newman/PhotoEdit. 21 middle row, left Michael Newman/PhotoEdit. 21 middle row, right Myrleen Ferguson/Photo Edit. 21 row 1, c.l. Michael Newman/Photo Edit. 21 row 1, c.r. Felicia Martinez/PhotoEdit. 21 row 1, l. Felicia Martinez/Photo Edit. 21 row 1, r. Myrleen Ferguson/PhotoEdit. 21 row 3, r. PhotoDisc. 31 bottom, left W.B. Spunbarg/Photo Edit. 31 bottom, right Ken Cavanagh. 31 t.l. Index Stock Photography, Inc. 31 t.r. Jose L. Pelaez/The Stock Market. 33 bottom, center D.Young-Wolff/PhotoEdit. 33 bottom, left Index Stock. 33 bottom, right PhotoDisc. 33 middle, center Chuck Savage/The Stock Market. 33 middle row, l. PhotoDisc, Inc. 33 row 1, l. Index Stock Photography. 33 top, center Gamma Liaison. 33 top row, r. PhotoDisc, Inc. 35 bottom, left Stock Works/The Stock Market. 35 bottom, right Dennis MacDonald. 37 bottom, left Tim Davis/Tony Stone Images. 37 middle, right Arthur Morris/ Visuals Unlimited. 37 row 1, l. Renee Lynn/Photo Researchers Inc. 37 row 2, m. PhotoDisc. 38 b. Thomas D. Mangelsen/Peter Arnold, Inc. 38 m. Stephen J. Krasemann/DRK Photo. 38 t. Wayne Lynch/DRK Photo. 41 row 1, c. L. West/Photo Reseachers, Inc. 41 row 1, l. Jonathan Nourok/Photo Edit. 41 row 1, r. Index Stock Photography. 41 row 2, c. Susan Van Etten/Stock Boston. 41 row 2, l. Raphael Macia/Photo Researchers, Inc. 41 row 3, c. Richard Pasley/Stock, Boston. 41 row 3, l. Daryl Balfour/Tony Stone Images. 41 row 3, l. Tim Davis/Photo Researchers inc. 43 bottom Michael Newman/Photo Edit. 43 top Michael Newman/Photo Edit. 51 b. Kamyar Shamouil. 53 row 1, l. Stock Boston. 53 row 1, m. B.Daemmrich/The Image Works. 53 row 2, l. D. Young-Wolff/Photo Edit. 53 row 2, m. Michael Keller/Stock Market. 53 row 3, l. SuperStock. 53 row 3, m. M. Ferguson/Photo Edit. 53 row 3, r. Joe Carini/The Image Works. 57 b.l. Bachmann/Index Stock Photography, Inc. 57 b.r. PhotoEdit. 57 m.l. Smith/Monkmeyer. 57 m.r. Susan Van Etten. 57 t.l. Ken Coleman/PhotoEdit. 57 t.r. PhotoEdit. 61 t. Tony Freeman/PhotoEdit. 65 m.l. Granitsas/The Image Works. 65 m.l. Roy Morsch/The Stock Market. 65 m.r. Gary Buss/FPG. 65 m.r. Jim Corwin/Stock Boston. 65 t.l. Gerard Lacz/Peter Arnold , Inc. 65 t.r. Axel-Jacana/Photo Researchers, Inc. 67 bottom Ariel Skelley/The Stock Market. 67 top David Young-Wolff/Photo Edit. 68 b.l. E.R. Degginger/Animals Animals. 68 b.r. Gregory G. Dimijian, M.D./Photo Researchers, Inc. 68 t.l. R.J. Erwin/DRK Photo. 68 t.r. Tom & Pat Leeson/DRK Photo. 69 b.l. David R. Frazier/Photo Researchers, Inc. 69 b.r. J. Taposchaner/ FPGInternational. 69 t.r. Bob Daemmrich/Stock Boston. 75 bottom, left Ken Cavanagh. 75 bottom, right Brian Stablyk/Tony Stone. 75 top, left Superstock. 75 top, right Bill Ivy/Tony Stone. 77 b. Tony Freeman/PhotoEdit. 77 t. Jim Cummins/FPG. 78 b. Eunice Harris/Photo Researchers, Inc. 78 m. Breck P.Kent/Animals Animals. 78 t. Stan Osolinski/FPG International 79 bottom, left George J. Sanker/DRK Photo. 79 bottom, right Tom McHugh/Photo Researchers. 79 top, left George J. Sanker/DRK Photo. 79 top, right Barbara Gerlach/DRK Photo. 80 bottom row, r. Ron Spomer/Visuals Unlimited. 80 row 1, l. Superstock. 80 row 1, m. Felicia Martinez/ Photo Edit. 80 row 1, r. John D.Cunningham/Visuals Unlimited. 80 row 2, c. George D.Lepp/Photo Researchers Inc. 80 row 2, l. Maslowski/Visuals Unlimited. 80 row 3, l. Stephen J Krasemann/Photo Researchers. 81 b. David Myers/Tony Stone Images. 81 t. Daniel J. Cox/Tony Stone Images. 82 row 1, l. Gregory K. Scott/Photo Researchers, Inc. 82 row 2, l. Leo Lause/Uniphoto Picture Agency. 82 row 2, r. David Woodfall/DRK Photo. 82 row 3, l. J.C. Carton/Bruce Coleman, Inc. 82 row 3, r. Superstock, Inc. 83 bottom Kennan Ward/The Stock Market. 83 top Tim Davis/The Stock Market. 85 b.l. A. & M. Shah/Animals Animals. 85 b.r. Jeff Lepore/Photo Researchers, Inc. 85 t.l. Dave B. Fleetham/Visuals Unlimited. 85 t.r. Suzanne L Collins & Joseph T Collins/Photo Researchers. 87 bottom, left Art Wolfe/Tony Stone. 87 bottom, right Ken Cavanagh. 87 top, left David Woodfall/Tony Stone. 87 top, right Index Stock Photography. 91 bottom Ariel Skelley/The Stock Market. 91 top, left Myrleen Ferguson/Photo Edit. 91 top, right Lorentz Gullachsen/Tony Stone. 101 t.r. Kamyar Shamouil. 103 row 2, r. Kevin Kolczynski for MHSD. 104 row 1, l. Ron Kimball/Ron Kimball Photography, Inc. 104 row 1, m. Ron Kimball/Ron Kimball Photography, Inc. 104 row 1, r.. Ron Kimball/Ron Kimball Photography, Inc. 104 row 2, l. John Daniels/Bruce Coleman, Inc. 104 row 2, m. Jeanne White/Photo Researchers, Inc. 104 row 2, r. John Daniels/Bruce Coleman, Inc. 104 row 3, l. John Daniels/Bruce Coleman, Inc. 104 row 3, m.l. Ron Kimball/Ron Kimball Photography, Inc. 104 row 3, m.r. Carolyn A. McKeone/Photo Researchers, Inc. 104 row 3, r. Larry Allen/Bruce Coleman, Inc. 104 row 3, r. Larry Allen/Bruce

Coleman, Inc. 106 row 1, l. J. & P. Wegner/Animals Animals. 106 row 1, r. Zefa Germany/The Stock Market. 106 row 2, l. Robert Maier/Animals Animals. 106 row 2, r. J. & P. Wegner/Animals Animals. 107 row 2, left Ian Royd/The Image Bank. 107 row 2, right Tim Davis/Photo Researchers, Inc. 108 row 1, l. Oswald Eckstein/Photo Researchers, Inc. 108 row 1, r. Index Stock Photography. 108 row 2, l. Patti Murray/Animals Animals. 108 row 3, l. Aaron Haupt/ Stock Boston. 108 row 3, r. SuperStock. 109 row 1, l. Felicia Martinez/Photo Edit. 109 row 1, m. Index Stock. 109 row 1, r. Michael Newman/Photo Edit. 109 row 2, c. Michael Newman/PhotoEdit. 109 row 2, l. Henry Ausloos/ Animals Animals. 111 t.l. Paul Hurd/Tony Stone Images. 115 row 3, l. Stuart Westmorland/Tony Stone Images, Inc. 115 row 3, m. Stuart Westmorland/Tony Stone Images, Inc. 115 row 3, r. Pete Turner/The Image Bank. 119 b.l. C Squared Studios/PhotoDisc, Inc. 119 b.r. Spencer Jones/FPG International. 119 t.r. Index Stock Photography. 123 b.r. Richard Hutchings/PhotoEdit. 123 m.l. Nancy Sheehan/PhotoEdit. 123 t.l. David Young-Wolff/ PhotoEdit. 123 t.r. Nancy Sheehan/PhotoEdit. 129 b.l. Ken Fisher/Tony Stone Images. 129 b.r. Gary Vestal/Tony Stone Images. 129 t.r. Ken Fisher/Tony Stone Images. 135 row 1, l. Tim Davis/Photo Researchers, Inc. 135 row 1, m. Ariel Skelley/The Stock Market. 135 row 1, r. Jim Cummings/FPG International. 135 row 2, l. David Hanover/Tony Stone Images. 135 row 2, m. Ariel Skelley/The Stock Market. 135 row 3, l. John M. Roberts/The Stock Market. 135 row 3, m. Don Mason/The Stock Market. 135 row 3, r. Gregory K. Scott/Photo Researchers, Inc. 137 t. Myrleen Ferguson/PhotoEdit. 138 b.l. Yoav Levy/Phototake/ PictureQuest. 138 t.r. Kindra Clineff /AllStock/PictureQuest. 139 t.l. Ken Cavanagh. 139 t.r. Ken Cavanagh. 147 m.l. Breck P.Kent / Animals Animals. 147 t.l. Ken Cavanagh. 153 m.r. David Woodfall/Tony Stone. 155 m.l. Myrleen Ferguson/PhotoEdit. ii b.l. Steve Cole/PhotoDisc. ii m. Kent Foster/Photo Researchers, Inc. ii t. G.W. Willis/Animals Animals. iii b.r. Siede Preis /PhotoDisc. iv b.l. Steve Cole/PhotoDisc.